ROB G. ADAMS

Win **FROM WITHIN**
DISCOVERING THE CHAMPION INSIDE

© Copyright 2018 Robert G. Adams III

Publisher: MBK Enterprises, LLC/Spotlight Publishing
Printed in the USA

ISBN 10: 1-7320727-3-6

ISBN 13: 978-1-7320727-3-2

Editor: Becky Norwood

Cover Design by: Chance Cessna

Cover Photography by: Chance Cessna

All rights reserved. No part of this book may be reproduced, stored in a retrieval system, or transmitted by any means, electronic, mechanical, photocopying, recording, or otherwise, without written permission from the author.

Rob G. Adams can be contacted at:
http://www.IAmRobGAdams.com

 @robgadams

 Rob G. Adams

 @robgadams

Table of Contents

ABOUT THE AUTHOR	v
DEDICATION	vii
CHAPTER 1 The Genesis	1
CHAPTER 2 Growing Up Fast	7
CHAPTER 3 It Takes Faith	23
CHAPTER 4 Overcome	41
CHAPTER 5 Discover the Champion Inside	47
FINAL THOUGHT	61
REFERENCES	67
LETTERS	69

ABOUT THE AUTHOR

Rob G. Adams, is an author, motivational speaker and life success coach with a deep passion for personal and spiritual growth. He has a unique story and has turned his pain into purpose so as to inspire others.

Born and raised in Brandon, Florida, "Rob" as family and friends affectionately call him, would later move to Northern Virginia for a period of time where he attended high school and college.

During his youth and into his adult life, he developed a love for sports and athleticism particularly in the areas of baseball and basketball. His mother played a vital role in Rob's development and encouraged him to stay focused and to keep God first. Rob was raised in a single parent home and understood from a young age the true meaning of responsibility.

Throughout high school and college, he found himself behaving like most young adults, following the crowd and seeking acceptance from surrounding peers. As a sophomore in college, Rob was living the college dream by being away from home and attending college parties. Soon, he would be faced with tackling treatments and making routine doctor visits due to an unexpected and sudden diagnosis of cancer. He was twenty years old.

To most, fighting cancer would appear to be a setback, but Mr. Adams decided to see it as a setup for something greater. After enduring nearly six months of intense treatments, he received the report of being completely cancer-free, and he continues to walk in his total healing.

Rob returned to college and finished what he started, earning his B.S. in business and is now involved in public speaking and various community-based activities. He is an inspiration to those around him and has proven that with God on your side, nothing is impossible!

Presently, he resides in Los Angeles, CA.

DEDICATION

Win from Within: Discovering the Champion Inside, is inspired by the memory of my beloved mother, Brenda Isaac-Adams, who showed me the importance of faith and the value of hard work.

CHAPTER 1
The Genesis

"The meaning of life is to find your gift. The purpose of life is to give it away."

—Pablo Picasso

As a child growing up in Brandon, Florida, I remember the excitement I had riding my brand new Huffy bike that I got for Christmas to the YMCA to shoot hoops and hangout with my with friends. This became one of my favorite pastimes after school. While in grade school, I remember the days of staring at the big white clock with black numbers posted above the whiteboard anxiously waiting for the bell to ring and for school to let out. "Have a good afternoon everyone and don't forget to study for your biology quiz on Friday!" "Quiz? Aw man!" I would reply jokingly. Of course, I'll arrange time to "study" later once I get home. However, I only thought about two things after school; not missing the bus, which seemed to happen on occasion and jumping on my new bike and burning rubber to get to the "Y."

I have fond memories of the times I spent at the "Y." From their engaging after-school programs to their fun and exciting summer camps, the "Y" became one of my favorite places to hangout growing up. I recall the times I participated in their annual "all-nighter." Every year around mid-July, the "Y" would host an all-night event for members family's, geared towards the youth and young adults. Now, this was no ordinary event! During an all-nighter, you can expect to hear music, find kids enjoying various games like twister and foosball, not to mention scarfing down all-you-can-eat pizza. During these special events, the "Y" also allowed kids access to the outdoor pool (until 10 p.m.) and play in what I describe as one of the best gymnastics foam pits on the east coast! Running, jumping and executing perfect cannonballs into this foam pit became not only a highlight of my night but of my childhood.

I felt free and it was the closest to flying that my young mind could conceive. Next to that would be a season pass to Busch Gardens and riding in the front row of every roller coaster that my younger sister and I could handle. "No-Hands!" we shout to one another as the roller coaster clicks-and-clacks its way up the steep vertical ascent. Deciding to get harnessed to a 75-mph thrill ride is daring but deciding to do it while sitting in the front row is sheer madness. I wouldn't have it any other way!

My passion for sports, particularly basketball, began to develop by the time I entered middle school. By this time, I demonstrated the basics of basketball from all the time I spent shooting hoops and playing in pick-up games at the "Y." I attended an average-sized middle school in the heart of Brandon, FL not

THE GENESIS

far from where my family and I lived at the time. I remember discussing with my mother, on several occasions, my desire to tryout and play basketball for my school's team. She supported all of my efforts and believed that I could do whatever I focused my mind to do. My mother's supportive nature was not only found during my athletic pursuits but also in my life in general. This is probably one of the most notable qualities about my mother. Her ability to remain supportive and to encourage my sisters and I to dream BIG.

My first basketball tryout is finally here and I feel pumped! The head coach goes over a few basics then begins tryouts by having everyone run full-court suicides to measure our conditioning. After a few suicides, we switch gears and, "coach" as many players called him, split everyone up into two teams for a full-court, 5-on-5 game. I mostly played between two positions in my youth and as a young teen; shooting guard and small forward. But, my personal favorite was playing the shooting guard position because I enjoyed shooting the ball whether mid-range or long-range. My shooting was solid throughout tryouts that day and my team was able to win both games to 21 points. I was even able to snag a few steals and collect a few assists in both games. Overall, I felt confident of my chances of making the team. Coach wrapped up tryouts with a round of hi-fives to all the players and told everyone the roster of new players would be posted in a few days.

WIN FROM WITHIN

REAL TALK

Sports can play a significant role in developing character, building work ethic, fostering teamwork and most importantly, teaching how to handle wins and losses. All of which, are vital qualities for success in real-life scenarios.

"Rob! Congratulations, you made the team, see you at practice!" shouted my coach down the hall as I was heading to the cafeteria. "Thanks coach!" I said with a huge smile. I remember the initial feeling I had of both excitement and accomplishment and I felt eager to get to practice that afternoon. I would later find out that I was the only black selected on the team out of a predominantly white school. I never felt discouraged or any less capable of performing. In fact, it made me want to work harder and develop my game even more. This became one of my first life lessons on how to win from within.

THE GENESIS

*At the end of each chapter is the **TAKE ACTION** section. Be sure to note your responses in the space provided below.*

TAKE ACTION

Take a moment and reflect on your early days of growing up. What memories come to mind? What advice would you share with your younger self?

_____

_____

_____

_____

_____

_____

_____

_____

_____

_____

_____

_____

CHAPTER 2
Growing Up Fast

"He who is not every day conquering some fear has not learned the secret of life."

—Ralph Waldo Emerson

Growing up in a single-parent home certainly didn't make my life any easier and brought with it, its own set of challenges. No question, my mother did her best to create as normal of an environment as possible for me as a child. I played outside with friends, paintball, attended state fairs for rides and funnel cake, rode my bike around until the street lights came on and just about anything else kids my age did. But, I still had to grow up a little faster than most of my surrounding peers. I had to learn early on the true meaning of responsibility and that life is not always fun and games. There's a level seriousness and focus that life demands. Some of the things my mother talked to me about as a kid, like how to be responsible, didn't seem all that important to an energetic young boy. She knew, however, that her insight would provide a strong foundation on which everything else in my life would be built.

The reality of my father's absence became amplified as I began to play sports. I remember the feeling I had of seeing many of my teammates working with their dads on different types of drills and exercises to sharpen their skills. The overall support these fathers provided to their sons was inspiring and made me want to be that type of dad one day. "Great shot, son!" or "Way to play good defense!" became common phrases I'd hear from the stands by these passionate fathers during games. As for me, my support system came mostly from the shouts of my mother and sisters as they cheered for me from the stands. My mother was supportive of all her children and seldom missed my games or failed to provide transportation to a young teen with a busy after-school schedule. Until, I was able to secure my own driver's license, then I wouldn't let her drive me anywhere; I thought I was grown!

Even with a dependable and loving mother by my side, nothing can fully substitute the presence of a good father. I do believe that a woman is able to raise a competent and strong male child under God's leadership and through leveraging positive male relationships. I am a product of such. However, the role of a good father is still a vital need in the household for both male and female children. There is something special that happens in the bond between a father and his children, particularly in the child's formative years. The love, support and overall value a good father adds to his home will leave a legacy for generations to come.

A father is more than a source for funding your extracurricular activities, more importantly, he is a tall sign of protection, guidance, encouragement and love to his home. In the article, *The Important Role of Dad*, human behavior and education expert, Dr. Gail Gross sheds light on the value of having a responsible father in the home: "studies show that if your child's father is affectionate, supportive and involved, he can contribute greatly to your child's cognitive, language and social development as well as academic achievement, a strong inner core resource, sense of well-being, good self-esteem and authenticity." Moreover, the role of a good father can help establish and reinforce a male child's sense of identity and self-worth. "Well-bonded boys develop securely with a stable and sustained sense of self."

REAL TALK

Just about any man can produce a child, that's the easy part. But, learning how to become a present and loving father that leads his home, requires a willing and committed man.

In my household growing up, my mother was at the helm navigating this thing called life with three children and a lot of faith. I have two immediate sisters: one younger and one older. Both are hard-working, intelligent and courageous. I grew up in the home mostly with my younger sister who has a big heart for music and animals, especially cats. I prefer dogs over cats because I think cats get temperamental and will unleash a fury of hissing and paws to the face for no apparent reason. Moreover, I feel like they're always up to something! Always watching and peeping around corners. But, I must say, I do find cats to be very funny animals. Infact, my sister and I can spend a good amount of time on the phone laughing at cat videos posted on YouTube.

Laughter runs in my family – literally. Isaac is my mother's maiden name which in Hebrew translates as, "he laughs" or more commonly known as, "laughter." In the biblical account of the story of Isaac starting in Genesis 17, we see God's promise to Abraham and Sarah of having their first-born child together. Abraham thought the whole idea of him and his wife bearing a child together at their 'seasoned' ages was quite humorous and they laughed at it (Genesis 17:17, 18:12). What were their ages you ask? Sarah was at the tender age of ninety and Abraham was one-hundred years old when they were first expected to give life (Genesis 17:17). Together, this remarkable couple had nearly two-hundred years of combined life experiences! This story serves as a constant reminder that **nothing** is impossible with God!

My mother played a large role in building and maintaining a positive, Christian home. She also cultivated a fun atmosphere and allowed me to be a kid! I remember many nights growing up where I spent my Friday nights going to the skating rink. Hanging out at the skating rink became one of my favorite things to do when I was in middle school. All of the 'cool kids' went to the skating rink including some the cute girls that I saw from around campus earlier in the week. It was a no brainer. Now, I was not much of a skater so I stayed occupied by hanging out with my friends, playing way too much pool and learning how to become comfortable around my female counterpart. At thirteen, my vocabulary with girls mostly ranged from, "Hi!" and "Do you like pizza?" Some may argue this still holds true to this day!

She also loved to cook and create tasty meals. Often, she would discuss with my sisters and I ahead of time of wanting to prepare a big dinner and that we could invite a friend over. She would then ask us what types of foods we wanted her to prepare. Whether it be her famous three cheese baked macaroni and cheese, or her Dr. Pepper baked beans made with actual Dr. Pepper soda, or maybe it was one of my personal favorites, her homemade sweet potato pie topped with vanilla bean ice cream. I really believe if God made anything better, He kept it to himself. I think my mother knew exactly what she was doing with all of this. She believed in the concept of family first and that reconciliation is more than just a word; it's a call to action. There can be so many underlying issues and misunderstandings within the family dynamic that if not solved, will only further divide and conquer. Cooking big meals became my mother's way of bringing my family together, or at least that was her greatest desire.

Coming home from practice to the aroma of a home-cooked meal was a part of the culture of my home growing up. Back then, I could bet that on nearly any given night, my mom would have something delicious cooked for dinner. At one point, she even entertained the idea of opening a small restaurant that would serve great food with quality customer service. My mother was a hard-working woman with a big heart for people. I believe that she enjoyed the art of service and making not only her family happy, but nearly anyone who came in contact with her. Even if it was through her smile and genuinely asking someone how their day is coming, she always had a way of making people feel special. People may forget what you say, but they'll never forget how you made them **feel.**

On several occasions in high school, my mom would have a summer or holiday cookout and tell me to invite my friends over for a plate. There was a basketball court down the street from where I lived while in high school. Some of my friends and I would play basketball there after we 'filled up our tank' with food from the cookout or throw the football around in the street out front of my townhome. No matter what we did on these days whether basketball or football, one thing is true: it was always good fun and better eating!

FINDING YOU

For most of my life growing up, attending church became a regular part of my Sunday mornings. Yet, for much of my youth and young adult life, I struggled to live my life centered around the principles I was learning every Sunday in church. In other words, I never really took church and the need to build my faith seriously. I figured since I was young, I have time to get things in order with God and that I have more important things to focus on right now. People-pleasing, fitting-in with the crowd and doing my own-thing 24/7 became a driving force in my life. I spent more time trying to be like my friends than I did trying to be like myself. I think many of us can relate, if we're honest.

I certainly wasn't a bad kid growing up, but like many, I struggled with finding and accepting myself. I followed more than I led. I didn't want the people that I hung around to label me as 'un-cool' so I found myself compromising in order to be liked. Through my very own struggles with acceptance from others growing up, I learned one valuable truth: You were never designed to blend in, fit in or look like those around you in the first place. You were created to be one-of-a-kind and there is no rival to being unique. There is more to you than meets the eye and it's time you start embracing all that God has put inside of you.

*Stop looking around and start looking **within**!*

Most people fail to live their best life because of fear, whether it's the fear of the unknown, the fear of failure, or the fear of rejection. Fear can have lasting and damaging effects in our lives and ultimately hinders us from reaching personal and professional achievement. In the article, *Overcoming the Crippling Effects of Fear*, Dontaira Terrell of the Huffington

Post, explains what fear is and provides practical tips on how to combat it. Fear, if not properly handled, "cripples decision-making, hinders success, promotions, finances and the ability to establish long lasting relationships." Furthermore, fear can present several types of physical manifestations: "it generates stress, anxiety, anger and ultimately leaves you powerless." So, how exactly can we loosen the grip of fear and operate in more faith?

There are several ways to beat or at least combat fear. For starters, learn to become your greatest encourager, not critic. Learning how to give yourself grace is one of the most important ways to overcome fear and negative thinking. If you make a mistake; examine what went wrong, make changes then move forward! Pay more attention to the things you do right and celebrate yourself along the journey. Rehearsing your mistakes and shortcomings every day and sitting in the mud of your own self-pity will never advance your life. If an almighty God can forgive and extend grace, why can't you?

Next, focus on your "why" in life. The answer to your why will serve as your strong conviction to get up every day and move forward in courage; not fear. Those who focus *more* on their why will subsequently focus *less* on fear. Everything you do and say needs to be directed not in reliving the past but on creating the future. Embrace your why as it will drive everything else that you do or don't do, achieve or do not achieve. Remember, where your mind goes your life will follow.

GROWING UP FAST

Lastly, just because you've failed at something in life, it doesn't mean that you're a failure! Truth is, everyone has failed at some point or another on their journey to success. I'd suggest that until you've failed or experienced failure, you haven't met the requirement for winning. It's a part of life and you have to overcome failure before you can move to your next level. Michael Jordan, has won 6 NBA championships and earned a staggering fourteen MVP awards among numerous other awards including, induction into the Naismith Memorial Basketball Hall of Fame class of 2009. But, even with a distinguished resume like Mr. Jordan's, it didn't make him exempt from let downs, disappointments or defeats. In the end, every challenge, setback and failure only further reveals the ***champion inside.***

> "I've missed more than 9,000 shots in my career. I've lost almost 300 games, 26 times I've been trusted to take the game-winning shot and missed. I've failed over and over and over again in my life. ***And that is why I succeed.***"
>
> —Michael Jordan

BIG CHANGES

By the time I transitioned into my first year of high school, my family and I had relocated to the D.C., Maryland and Virginia area or, as locals call it, the DMV. The change in weather was one of the first things I noticed and I purchased my first real winter jacket after moving to the DMV. Track jackets, basketball shorts and T-shirts may not do the job in the dead of winter here. At least, not for me. I thought I understood cold weather until January came around and I'd have to scrape ice off our car windshield before early morning commutes to work and school. Waking up to twenty-five-degree weather and wind chills that made my eyes water became a common occurrence during the winter months. Good times!

Living in the DMV also gave me my first chance of seeing snow. My very first winter gave me the opportunity of experiencing snow and all the beauty that comes along with it. I thought the view from our living room window was nothing shy of amazing. Several inches of fresh, powder-like snow covered the sidewalks, cars, neighbor's rooftops and I even saw a dog leaping up to catch snowflakes as they fall. I will never forget the fun and beauty of my first time experiencing snow.

Having the opportunity of living close to the nation's capital was very exciting and I wanted to make the most out of this experience. I remember the first time I got a chance to visit the Lincoln Memorial, the Jefferson Memorial and the massive Washington Monument located on the National Mall. I even had a chance to visit the recently constructed thirty-foot statue of Dr. Martin Luther King Jr., which faces the Tidal Basin. One of the most remarkable aspects about this statue is the 450-foot long Inscription Wall that displays fourteen quotes from Dr. King's sermons, speeches and writings. No matter which statue or memorial you visit, each of these pieces of iconic American history have so much depth and carry a presence of their own.

I attended a fairly large high school in Ashburn, VA about an hour outside of Washington, D.C. I remember my first day of high school as both exciting and nerve-racking. Like most, I seemingly admired the upper-classmen and thought they were cool, especially those on sports teams. I perceived a few of these guys as having swag, well-dressed and confident. I also noticed how both girls and guys wanted to be around these athletes. It was effortless. When you operate in your gift, people want to be around you. There is something attractive about those who decide to do something with their life. Most of us enjoy being around that type of energy; it inspires us. An athlete is only one example.

From a young age, I grew up playing sports and being athletic. I played baseball for several years when I was younger and noticeably becoming a good outfielder due to my overall throwing mechanics and ability to track fly balls. In fact, one summer while in middle school, I was invited to go to camp with other skilled players in the area. The camp was held at the University of Tampa in downtown Tampa, Florida and I found it to be a terrific experience. But, even with a demonstrated ability in baseball, I still gravitated back to basketball and it eventually became my one ambition. While in high school, I would spend hours in the gym (by myself sometimes) practicing various types of drills; setting up cones for footwork, ball handling and jump shooting exercises. Not to mention, playing in open gyms and pick-up games at local recreation centers.

No matter how bad I wanted it or how much I practiced on my game, playing basketball for my high school was just not meant to be. However, I remained upbeat and continued playing in other leagues throughout high school to keep my competitive edge.

At the time, never being able to play basketball for my high school team made me feel very discouraged. Each year presented another season and another opportunity for me to compete and tryout, but my name was never listed on the roster. One major take-away for me by not making my high school basketball team is that it ignited the will to never quit. Early on - I learned how to dig deep from within and gather the courage and strength to keep fighting for what I wanted.

Little did I know at the time that learning how to dig deep from within would later serve as a great resource in what will soon be the fight of my life.

As writer, Stanley Lindquist explains it:

> *"God allows us to experience the low points of life, to teach us lessons we could not learn in any other*

way. The way we learn those lessons is not to deny the feelings but, to find the meanings underlying them."

TAKE ACTION

Finding out what your unique talents, abilities and skill sets are is one of the greatest discoveries you will ever make. More important than noticing what others are capable of doing, is learning how to examine and cultivate your very own potential within. Embrace the undeniable qualities that make you, you.

What are your unique skill sets and talents?

_____

_____

_____

_____

_____

_____

_____

_____

_____

_____

_____

GROWING UP FAST

What steps are you taking today to advance your potential?

_____
_____
_____
_____
_____
_____
_____

Are you overly concerned about what people think of you? Why or why not?

_____
_____
_____
_____
_____
_____
_____
_____

CHAPTER 3
It Takes Faith

"Life is not about how hard you hit but how hard you can get hit and keep moving forward."

—Sylvester Stallone, *Rocky Balboa*

In just a few months, I will complete my sophomore year of college and head home for summer break. It was around this time that I first began to have persistent headaches. It seemed like nearly every other day during the final months of my spring semester I experienced a headache. I'd take a pain reliever, only to experience a headache returning in a few hours, or the next day. I called my mother who was back home and described to her what I was experiencing. She recommended that I make an appointment with an ENT (Ear, Nose, and Throat) specialist. Once I returned home for my summer break I went to see a doctor. After three visits with an ENT specialist they realized they needed to investigate further. The doctor then conducted a procedure called a nasal endoscopy to see in the back of my nostrils and throat. She was able to identify a small mass located in the upper part of my right nostril in the area referred to as the nasopharynx. She recommended that I get a biopsy to find out more about the mass. Only a few days after my biopsy, the results came in:

WIN FROM WITHIN

REAL TALK

Words can't begin to express the rush of questions that came over me as I waited for the results from the biopsy to come back. What would it reveal? Would it come back as cancer?

I could feel my heartbeat pounding through my chest as the doctor began to discuss the results with my family and I. "I'm sorry, Mr. Adams but the biopsy revealed that you have cancer and we need to start treatments immediately." I simply couldn't believe what I was hearing that afternoon! "How could this happen to me? I'm healthy, I exercise regularly and I'm only twenty years old?" were the first thoughts that came to mind as I intently listened to the doctor explain his findings. As I looked over to my family, I noticed my mother grabbing a tissue from her purse and patting under her eyes as we hugged one another. Surprisingly, I never once remember crying in the doctor's office that day. I respected the doctor's medical opinion as well as his advice on my treatments in the months ahead. However, I had enough faith in God to believe that this seemingly insurmountable giant wouldn't be the end of my story! Something deep within my soul enabled me to take a deep breath, remain calm and tackle what will be intense months of cancer treatments head on.

During my initial consult with my oncologist, I learned about the type of cancer I had, and the necessary treatments that would give me the best chance of beating it. His office was very surprised to see an otherwise, healthy young man, with this rare type of cancer. Nearly every office I visited during this time had qualified and attentive staff that were ready to take the necessary steps to get me on the road to recovery. My primary oncologist handled my blood work, scheduling of treatments, weight management, and any additional concerns that I had. Since I required radiation treatments, I would also have a radiation oncologist alongside my primary oncologist. Together, they developed the best plan for my care in what will be arduous months ahead.

THE RAIN

My first radiation treatment commenced on ***August 9, 2007.*** I entered the office, and the office manager waved to me from behind the sliding glass window. She then notified the tech of my arrival, and that I was ready to begin my first treatment. Her greeting became standard with most patients entering the office. It was almost as if waving to her was our way of saying, "We're here and ready to conquer this thing!"

My mother and I would sit in the lobby until I was called back by the tech. If there were no delays, she would normally wait a total of twenty minutes from start to finish. Once I reached the machine, the tech instructed me to enter the changing room and remove my shirt, pants, and any jewelry, and then put on a gown, before starting each treatment. I remember seeing a large mirror hanging in the changing room where I'd look at myself from time to time. On occasion, I would stare into this mirror, and say something positive, or simply remind myself that I'm going to make it!

As a result of the intense treatments, my physical body begins to experience significant changes. *Make no mistake; I didn't look strong and in shape!* I had lost a good amount of muscle mass from not being able to work out on a regular basis. My appetite also got considerably low, which means I didn't eat on a regular basis. I needed to drink both high-protein and high-calorie shakes to help supplement for what I wasn't able to get through eating a balanced diet. Some of these nutritional shakes we bought at the grocery store by popular brands like Boost and Ensure.

My mother often created delicious homemade smoothies filled with nutrient rich ingredients like: whey protein, blueberries, glutamine, almond milk and chia seeds to name a few. During my experience with cancer, my mother and I began to research powerful foods that are nutrient rich and full of antioxidants (substances that may prevent or delay cell damage). One of the best ways to prevent and fight against sickness is by eating a healthy diet. There are plenty of resources online that dive deeper into how to build and maintain a healthy diet. I strongly encourage anyone going through a medical issue to begin researching foods that combat the issue at-hand. Since my experience with cancer, I have decided to develop a more plant-based diet with little to no processed foods including meat, dairy and other animal-based products. This decision has completely revolutionized my life and my body for the better! I experience higher energy levels, my mind is more alert and sharp and I even sleep more consistently throughout the night. Eating healthy is not an option, it is your only option if you want to not only survive but thrive. Start taking steps towards better eating habits today and your body will thank you later.

REAL TALK

Everything I was facing in these arduous months, would press every ounce of faith and inner strength that I had on the inside. I had to learn how to Win from Within.

As I walked out of the changing room and into the treatment room, several techs greeted me. "Hey man, what's up!?" one asked with a smile. "Not too much!" I replied with a laugh. The high-tech and innovative method of delivering the radiation I received is called tomotherapy. It's a form of Intensity Modulated Radiation Therapy that integrates a CT scan into the treatment to better target the mass, and reduce radiation to healthy tissue. The scan allows greater precision for the radiation treatment by pinpointing the mass.

After the CT scan, the tech came back into the room, made a few minor adjustments to the table, then shouted, "Here we go!" As my treatment began, I would often close my eyes and try to relax. It was during this time, that I learned how to find that place of inner peace and put my mind in a positive place.

On most occasions, treatment from start to finish only lasted about twenty minutes. I could hear the machine quieting down as the generator turned off, and the table slowly returning to the original height. "Ok, Mr. Adams…all done. Everything looks good, see you tomorrow!" the tech said. "Ok great, see you tomorrow," I replied. I repeated this same process every day, Monday through Friday for just over two months.

I would change back into my original T-shirt and sweatpants then head out the double doors to the lobby where I meet with my mother. I would then go home to rest for the remainder of the afternoon due to my overall lack of energy. My *faith* remains that God will meet me at the finish line.

The following Monday afternoon I would be back at the office for another treatment. "Honestly, I don't want to be here today, because I feel weak and nauseous" was the thought I had coming into the office that day. Some days became harder than other days, but I somehow manage to gather the strength to continue treatment. I don't recall crying much from the initial diagnosis to the start of treatments, but this day was different. While sitting in the lobby waiting to be called back, I begin to sink down in my seat, and with my sunglasses on, I begin to tear up. I think it was at this point that I began to realize just how long this road would be.

IT TAKES FAITH

REAL TALK

A lot of growth can happen when it's just you, yourself and I. These places can seem lonely, but they are known to build faith, character, strength, and reveal your true heart.

As the tech prepared the machine for my treatment, I noticed a small radio sitting on the counter behind the tomotherapy machine. Often the techs would turn on the radio or play a CD for me as the treatments were given. The music would play softly in the background and I found it to be very soothing. In fact, during each treatment, I would close my eyes and rest for about 10 minutes or so to the sounds of saxophonist Kenny G, or some other jazz artist.

During this time, I began to question why God allowed me to experience all of this. I'm young, otherwise healthy and in the prime of my life. I just don't understand any of it!

As I left the treatment room, I was greeted by a woman who is assigned to my overall care and will make routine follow-ups on my progress. I did my best to remain positive and carry a pleasant spirit during my treatments. Some of the people in her office looked at me with both puzzled and amazed expressions, "How can he be this pleasant?" Another said, shaking her head, "He's so young!" I recall the times where a nurse would mention how they have a son or daughter that is my age, and how difficult it must be for both the parent and child to go through all of this. I had firsthand experience of what I saw and felt in my own body, yet I had to make a decision. I can decide to look through the eyes of hope or I can decide to look through the eyes of my temporary reality.

Coming up on my final few radiation treatments, I felt what I thought was a tsunami from all of the treatments. I was originally 188lbs starting out but my weight reached an all-time low of 146lbs during these last few treatments. In total, I lost over 40lbs of muscle mass in just 3 months! The total effect of the radiation treatments made my energy very low and I found myself struggling to complete routine tasks. Daily tasks like showering, brushing my teeth, getting dressed, and even eating, all became very challenging during this time. Thankfully, my mother was a nurse and her advice and guidance became pivotal in my maintenance and later full recovery. I even reached a point where I could not sleep for more than 3 hours straight, so I began taking a sleep aid to help me get a decent night's rest. During this time, I preferred to sleep on one of the couches in our living room rather than sleeping in my own bed. I found the couch to be more comfortable while putting me closer to the things I needed downstairs on the kitchen counter.

BETTER DAYS

Around this time, I heard about my family having an upcoming reunion. I did not feel well enough to go, but I gathered

IT TAKES FAITH

some strength and accompanied my mother and sister to the reunion. Thinking back, I'm really glad I went, because it turned out to be a fun time with family and friends. My family decided to have the reunion at Hains Point in Washington, D.C., a spacious park area off the Potomac River with room for volleyball, picnics and many other outdoor activities. Many of my family members were present on that warm, summer afternoon. For some of them, this would be my first time seeing face-to-face. I remember my, at the time, 10-year-old cousin's son grabbing an open spot on the picnic table next to me and asking, "Robby...are you ok?" I paused for a minute and replied with a smile, "Yeah, Robby is ok." He then squints his eyes and asks, "When are we going to play basketball again?" With a laugh and a high five I respond, "We'll shoot hoops soon!" Satisfied, he ran to his friends and continued playing.

Meanwhile, I look over at my uncles who are managing the grill, and all I could see was a grill racked with chicken, burgers, and ribs. My spirit and appetite lifted a bit more. I noticed that on the picnic tables were various macaroni dishes, potato salad, a few different pies, fruit salad, dinner rolls, salads, and juices. I saw the food, and trust me, I wanted to enjoy it, but I could not enjoy a single piece of it. From all the treatments and lack of energy, my appetite is non-existent. It was during this time that most foods tasted like cardboard. Weight management is so important because it is hard to eat when you have no desire to eat. Nonetheless, I fixed a small plate and as

WIN FROM WITHIN

I took a bite of the burger, I began to recall how incredible a hamburger tastes with all the trimmings.

The quote by the great American writer James Thurber inspires me: *"He was always leaning forward, pushing something invisible ahead of him."*

I completed my treatments and Christmas Day is right around the corner. This year, my mother and sister assembled our Christmas tree with multi-colored lights, ornaments and angel tree topper. As my family decorated and set the atmosphere for Christmas, I sat in my favorite chair watching and engaging in conversation. I was beyond happy to be spending Christmas Day with my family, and watching our home come alive for the holidays. I saw a few presents under the Christmas tree and figured I would try to sneak-a-peak, you know, peel away the smallest corner of wrapping paper hoping to reveal the gifts.

Unfortunately, the gifts were hidden near the backside of the tree, and unreachable to my sister and I. Mom won again. It seemed like every time around Christmas my mother became an expert gift hider. Like a Christmas gift ninja, making everything a complete surprise the next morning. For most of my childhood, I rarely saw presents under the Christmas tree before Christmas Day. Every Christmas, I thought Santa/my mom forgot to get her wonderful children presents. Well, I was wrong, she remembered. She just hid them in various places until Christmas morning to heighten the suspense. Way to go, mom!

IT TAKES FAITH

December 25, 2007, is finally here and today marks Christmas Day. My family and I are in the living room about to open gifts. For me, this Christmas is very special. Beyond being able to spend it with my family. After enduring nearly 6 months of intense medical treatments for a rare diagnosis of nasopharynx cancer, I'm confidently looking forward to greater days ahead. As I start to open gifts on that beautiful Christmas Day morning, I can't help but be grateful for one of the greatest gifts of all. The gift of life!

With the New Year fast approaching, I began to recap on this truly unforgettable and life-changing year I've had. I was an otherwise healthy young man growing up that was diagnosed with cancer at the peak of my young adult life. My experience would allow me to embark on a difficult journey both personally and spiritually unlike anything I have ever experienced before. My faith was tested, my courage was strengthened and as a direct result, something greater has awakened from within.

According to Merriam-Webster's dictionary, faith is described as: *"Something that is believed especially with strong conviction. Complete trust or confidence in someone or something."*

The definition never mentioned that faith fluctuates based on present feelings or how well you understand the situation. Faith would not be faith if we understood everything and had an answer for all that happens in our lives. Simply put, faith requires full and complete confidence. In the words of civil rights activist and minister Dr. Martin Luther King Jr., *"Faith is taking the first step even when you don't see the whole staircase."*

Here's an interesting conversation about God between a barber and his customer. The story takes place in a typical barbershop:

A man went to a barbershop to have his haircut and his beard trimmed. As the barber began to work, they began to have a good conversation. They talked about many things and various subjects.

When they eventually touched on the subject of God, the barber said:

"I don't believe that God exists."

"Why do you say that?" asked the customer.

"Well, you just have to go out in the streets to realize that God doesn't exist.

Tell me, if God exists, would there be so many sick people? Would there be abandoned children?

If God existed, there would be neither suffering nor pain.

I can't imagine a loving God who would allow all of these things."

The customer thought for a moment but did not respond because he did not want to start an argument.

IT TAKES FAITH

The barber finished his job, and the customer left the shop.

Just after he left the barbershop, he saw an average person with long, stringy, dirty hair and an untrimmed beard. He looked dirty and unkept.

The customer turned back and entered the barber shop again, and he said to the barber:

"You know what? Barbers do not exist."

"How can you say that?" asked the surprised barber.

"I am here, and I am a barber. And I just worked on you!"

"No!" the customer exclaimed. "Barbers don't exist because if they did, there would be no people with dirty long hair and untrimmed beards, like that man outside."

"Ah, but barbers DO exist! That's what happens when people do not come to me."

"Exactly!" affirmed the customer. "That's the point! God, too, DOES exist!

That is what happens when people do not go to Him and do not look to Him for help.

That's one reason why there's so much pain and suffering in the world."

The reason why there is so much pain and trouble in the world is because people fail to surrender their lives to God and ask for help. Until we can become humble enough to express a need for Him, we will continue dealing with problems today that He could have solved yesterday.

TAKE ACTION

Any medical diagnosis, especially one of cancer, can be a life-changing experience for the individual diagnosed and for those closest to them. Has anyone close to you, including yourself, ever received a medical diagnosis? If so, who?

_____

_____

_____

_____

Describe your initial reactions and feelings after the diagnosis?

_____

_____

_____

_____

_____

_____

_____

_____

WIN FROM WITHIN

Do you believe that God has a plan for your life? Why or why not?

_____
_____
_____
_____
_____
_____
_____

Do you believe that God loves and cares about you? Why or why not?

_____
_____
_____
_____
_____
_____
_____

IT TAKES FAITH

If you're currently facing a medical issue, create a list of 3 positive declarations to speak over your health. Write them in the space below. I encourage finding a few Bible verses on healing and faith. Also, read stories of how God healed different people with different needs in scripture. Read them often as this will increase your faith that the same thing or BETTER can happen for YOU!

CHAPTER 4
Overcome

"Strength doesn't come from what you can do. It comes from overcoming the things you once thought you couldn't."

—Rikki Rogers

On the afternoon of *January 22, 2008*, I arrived at my oncologist's office for a routine PET scan. I was beginning to feel much better by this time, and I could see things gradually starting to return to normal in my body. My strength is coming back, and I was able to do more on my own without any assistance. I walked into the doctor's office and waved, as usual, then grabbed a seat in the lobby and waited to be called for my scan.

I picked up a TIME Magazine from the coffee table and began to read a few articles for what seemed like an eternity. Finally, I heard my name called, so I walked to the back area where my scan took place. The tech briefly explained the purpose of the scan, then began to prepare my arm for the injection.

My mother and I got along very well with my doctors and nurses, and it showed. On several occasions, I'd see her sharing laughs and having conversations with my nurses and office manager as I was receiving treatment. After the scan is complete and the oncologist has a chance to review everything, I'll receive a phone call explaining the results of my scan. Although, I already know the results…by faith!

On this occasion, two days passed, I had not heard anything from the oncologist regarding my PET scan results. My mother and I had a few errands to run earlier that afternoon, so we returned to the house around 4 p.m. After we returned home, I did what I normally do when I get home; go to the fridge, scurry around for food, then head upstairs to my room. As I'm about to turn on my TV, I hear my mom shout from the living room, "Someone left a voicemail from the doctor's office…I'll check it." I didn't give what she said much thought as I figured it was just like every other voice message. Well, this one was different.

As my mom begins to listen to the message, an overwhelming sense of joy comes over her, and she begins to scream. My first thought was, "Did we win the lottery?" I didn't realize what was going on, so she hands me the phone, "You've got to hear this…it's for you!" I put the phone to my ear and begin to walk into the kitchen. It was from my oncologist's office. One of my nurses requested that I return her call immediately so that she could give me the results of the scan. She sounded extremely happy and eager to deliver the news. As soon as I called the office and said my name, my nurse shouted, "Robert…it's all gone, Congratulations!!"

I began to express my appreciation to everyone at the office, when I heard the voice of my oncologist in the background, "Robert…it is completely gone, and you are on your way… Congratulations!" As I hung up the phone that afternoon, I felt an incredible sense of peace and accomplishment. My mother had tears in her eyes as I began to make phone calls to my family and friends about the good news!

*"Let the redeemed of the Lord **say so…**"* - Psalm 107:2

FAITH WORKS

One of my favorite examples of the faith that heals is the woman described in Mark 5:25-34. Here we see a woman who has suffered an issue of blood for twelve years. She visited many doctors, and yet her issue never saw improvement, in fact, it grew worse! (Mark 5:26). This woman had enough faith that God could heal her, and that's exactly what He did. In Mark 5:34, we see Jesus telling her that her faith has healed her and to go in peace. What an amazing story of the faith that heals. Remarkable things can happen when you believe!

But, how do I put my faith in something I can't see or touch?

Think about the last time you drove your car somewhere. Maybe the last time you drove to work or picked up a few items from the grocery store. Did you ever question if your car would start? Or how about the last time you sat in a chair at work, or in your home office, or at a restaurant for a dinner party with friends, did you ever wonder if the chair would break from under you, leaving you helplessly laying on the floor? Most of us probably answered, "Of course not!"

One thing is true: Whether we get in our cars to go grocery shopping, or grab a seat at a table, we demonstrate a very basic level of faith or belief that these things will perform and support our daily lifestyle. We drive our cars and sit in chairs every single day without thinking twice. It's second nature. I have yet to see someone ask for the latest service report of an elevator before they enter. So, how can we so effortlessly put our faith in small things yet struggle to trust God?

REAL TALK

One illustration puts it this way, "The best way to see God is through the lives of people. In how He changes and transforms lives." Incredible things will happen, as God becomes an active part of your everyday life.

My strength and overall bodily performance began to increase. My appetite is increasing with each day and I can enjoy the flavor of my favorite foods again. Gradually, my life began to

OVERCOME

return to normal and I'm able to rebuild and regain everything that was temporarily lost. I work out on a regular basis, eat a balanced diet and make time for various athletic activities. Some of my favorite activities include playing basketball, throwing the football with friends and jogging the scenic hills of Runyon Canyon Park in Los Angeles, CA. I even picked up where I left off and completed my bachelor's degree in business from Liberty University. My life's message is simple: With God on your side, nothing is impossible!

What do you want your life's message to be?

TAKE ACTION

The word overcome is described as, "to succeed in dealing with a problem or difficulty; to defeat an opponent, prevail." Take a moment and think about a time when you overcame something in your own life. Try to recall a recent experience. How did it make you feel to overcome?

CHAPTER 5
Discover the Champion Inside

Let's checkout three important concepts that I exercised and attribute to my healing and restoration from cancer. I believe that each of these concepts are fundamental to WIN over any challenge that comes your way.

Faith

The unwavering belief that God is able to do something in your life.

> "Without **faith** it is impossible to please God, anyone who comes to Him must believe that He exists..."
>
> —Hebrews 11:6

> "Faith is all about believing. You don't know how it will happen. You just know that it will."
>
> —Unknown

Faith is one of the most important concepts that I wanted to exercise during my experience with cancer. Whether it was through what I said around others or in my private time in prayer, I never wanted to entertain doubt even if others had doubt. I had to fully believe that God was able and willing to heal my body.

Often easier said than done, trusting in God's plan regardless of how things "appear," will challenge and stretch us in ways nothing else can. How do I believe in something I can't see? Faith is the belief that as I take my step, God will take His. Believing that God is able to meet you at your point of need is the first step to growing in faith. Dr. Dennis Kimbro, author of Think and Grow Rich: A Black Choice explains it this way, *"Believing is the beginning of faith. When the force of faith is unleashed, power becomes unlimited and possibilities are without end."*

Faith is the vehicle that transports things into the physical equivalent. If you ever want to see something in your life; good health, the right relationships, etc., you have to exercise a strong belief that you **can** lay hold of these things! Be intentional and exercise the belief that good things are destined for your life no matter how things may appear in your life today. This is what the essence of faith is all about. From Dr. Kimbro, "When you truly believe and comprehend this attribute, putting it into action, you may then control or at least be able to adjust to every setback or negative experience in your life."

Faith operates similarly to a muscle in how it gains strength through daily, repeated use. Think about the last time you exercised at your local gym. The more consistently you train your muscles through exercise, the stronger and better they begin to look, feel and respond. With time and healthy eating habits, your muscles can become very strong and your physical appearance can begin to transform before your eyes. Your entire body begins to change and you can handle a more intense workout than when you first started. It's no different when it comes to your faith muscle. The more you build your faith muscle through reading scriptures, attending service and doing things that will energize and invigorate your faith, the more developed this muscle becomes. Things that use to bother, worry and upset you, now do not even ruffle your feathers or break your stride. You have come to the realization that God's got your back and He will never let you down. If He brought you to it, He will bring you ***through*** it!

REAL TALK

Touch God with your faith, and He will touch you with His power.

WIN FROM WITHIN

The Power of Words

What you decide to say about yourself and your life matters!

"The tongue has the power of life and death."

—Proverbs 18:21

"Words are containers for power. You choose what kind of power they carry."

—Joyce Meyer

"Realize now the power that your words command if you simply choose them wisely."

—Tony Robbins

Words are seeds and seeds are *living* things! Every time you say something whether positive or negative, "I'm a failure," or "I'm going to make it," you are planting seeds that will eventually become your reality.

Boxing legend, Muhammad Ali is highly respected for not only his quick footwork and ability to navigate around punches in the ring, but also for his wit and bold affirmations in the face of his opponents. Ali was able to exude this type of confidence even in the face of contenders who were bigger and stronger with the odds of a win in their favor.

Some of his most recognized statements include, "I am the greatest," and "Float like a butterfly, sting like a bee." One of my favorite quotes from Muhammad Ali that reveals how speaking positively can have a direct impact on your life:

"It's the repetition of affirmations that leads to belief. And once that belief becomes a deep conviction, things begin to happen."

Ali understood the value of words and unleashing the power of positive confessions. Even when his back was against the wall, and it appeared that an opponent had the upper hand. He continued to speak positive, strong, bold statements throughout his career. His positive confessions got into the minds of his opponents so much so that it would throw them off their game. They became so enraged by Ali's confidence and outspoken nature, that by the time the actual fight happened, they would tire themselves out early in the fight from over throwing punches. In addition, trying to catch Ali around the ring was no easy task due to his exceptional footwork and ability to maneuver around punches with finesse. Ali capitalized on this tactic throughout his career, making him one of the greatest boxers of all time.

As I was going through cancer, I made every effort to respond to my nurses as positively as possible. I gave responses like,

"I'm doing well," or "I'm going to make it," when asked how I was doing on a particular day. Of course, I had my fair share of days when all I wanted to do was hang-out in bed and rest, but even then, I still wanted to remain as upbeat as possible and only discuss positive things. It's in times of difficulty that standing on the truth of God's word provides a wellspring of strength, encouragement and hope unlike anything else can. During this time, I meditated and focused on scriptures that dealt with my current situation: my health. (Isaiah 53:5, John 11:4, Romans 8:28).

No matter what you are facing today, understand that the words you speak, have direct power in your life. Make the conscious decision to speak positive declarations over yourself and your life. Stand on God's word and realize that one of your most creative weapons is your mouth!

What do you want to see grow in your life?

DISCOVER THE CHAMPION INSIDE

Attitude determines Altitude

Be determined to see the good in every situation regardless of the outcome.

"If you change the way you look at things, the things you look at change."

—Dr. Wayne Dyer

"Ability is what you are capable of doing. Motivation determines what you do. Attitude determines how well you do it."

—Lou Holtz

REAL TALK

Understand that you don't have the power to control what happens to you. None of us do. However, what each of us do have is the power of decision-making. Decide today how you will respond to things that happen in your life. Use everything to advance positive change in your life!

Attitude goes hand-in-hand with using positive confessions. How you view the world around you and more importantly yourself, can play a major role in your attitude and your outlook on life. "I'm going to make it." "Today was tough, but tomorrow will be better," or you can decide to allow things to cause ongoing damage to your life long after it happened. "I'll never find someone special." "Only bad things seem to happen to me." These words lack empowerment. You have the power to shape the world around you, and it starts with your attitude. I've had the chance to live in several different cities in my life and meet people from all lifestyles. I find that many people have talent, but for some, their ***attitude*** hinders their progress. A negative attitude has the same effect as putting a lid on a container.

Think about the last time you put a lid on something. A lid serves two purposes: to keep what's inside, in and to keep what's outside, out. Carrying around a negative, self-destructive attitude will only create separation from all that you have on the inside (your purpose, talents, gifts) from all the beautiful things that exist on the outside (key relationships both professional and personal).

The Law of Attraction suggests that each of us will attract whatever our minds focus on. In other words, you are a human magnet constantly attracting or repelling things in your life based on your thought life! You can create whatever you want for your life, and it all begins with your thoughts.

What do you want to create?

I recall watching a clip of an interview with actor and comedian, Jim Carrey on the Oprah show early in his career. In the interview,

DISCOVER THE CHAMPION INSIDE

Mr. Carrey explains something that he did that I thought was both bold and eye-opening. Like most young actors early in their career, Mr. Carrey had no money but had talent and a dream. He recalls the time he drove his car to Mulholland Drive in Beverly Hills simply to remind himself that, "these things are out here (nice homes, luxury cars, etc.) I just don't have them yet."

Early on, Mr. Carrey practiced visualizing what he wanted, and eventually, that's exactly what he got. He didn't allow his attitude to become negative in the midst of his present way of life. Instead, he decided to remain upbeat, and as time unfolds, his situation drastically changed. The part of his interview that I want us to focus on is when he shared the story of when he wrote himself a check for *ten million dollars.* The check was for, "acting services rendered," and then gave himself a timeline of five years to earn the money. He dated the check and slipped it into his wallet.

He begins to describe how over the years the check began to deteriorate and become old from day-to-day living. Only days before his 5-year deadline, on Thanksgiving 1995, Mr. Carrey finds out that he will be making ten million dollars from the movie he stared in with actor Jeff Daniels, *Dumb and Dumber.*

Mr. Carrey goes on to say,

"I believe we're all creators, we all have the ability to create. With every thought, every word, and every moment."

WIN FROM WITHIN

Renowned TV host, comedian, and author, Steve Harvey sheds light on this subject while on his daytime TV show, *Steve Harvey*. Mr. Harvey discusses a few concepts with the audience that helped him achieve success, particularly in television.

Let's take a look at a few of these concepts. The first one is:

Like attracts Like: Mr. Harvey explains the idea that we are like magnets in that we attract whatever we are. If you are negative, you will attract negative people. If you are positive, you will attract positive people. If you are kind, more people are kind to you and so on. Furthermore, he believes that each of us needs to have a vision and a sense of direction in life. You will never have what you are unwilling to see yourself capable of having. There is something powerful about vision.

REAL TALK

"If you see it in your mind, you can hold it in your hands. You have to create a vision board. Put your favorite car up on your mirror at home. Put a picture of the waist size you want to be, in the refrigerator."

The next concept is: ***Ask, Believe, Receive.*** Mr. Harvey believes many of us tend to overlook this one. We get discouraged if we don't have all the answers and are unable to map everything out in our lives. He reminds the audience that feeling like this is normal, but we should not allow the feeling of discouragement to hinder us from moving forward.

"You don't have to know how. You have to ask, believe, and receive. That's as simple as it gets."

The final concept is to always show: **Gratitude.**

Showing gratitude for where you currently are is important because it keeps you levelheaded. There's nothing wrong with wanting better for yourself, or for those around you, but make sure it doesn't take away from you enjoying the present. There are stages in your life, just like there are stages of your human development (infant, toddler, child, adolescent, etc.) You were not automatically born an adult. It took time, growth, development, pain, experiences and finding yourself before you became an adult. Your life is a constant process. I believe those who experience the most fulfillment in life, are those who learn how to be grateful and value the gift of a brand-new day! Furthermore, I believe that living a grateful life can help combat feelings of depression and suicide. Take a moment to reflect on your life and consider just how fortunate you really are. Not to sound cliché, but things could have been worse. Someone may be praying for the things you already have! The take home is clear, developing an attitude of gratitude will not only help you reach your next level but help you to enjoy the journey along the way.

WIN FROM WITHIN

"The only way you can move to the next level is to show gratitude for where you are. If you show gratitude, you'll get to where you want to be faster."

DISCOVER THE CHAMPION INSIDE

TAKE ACTION

Create a list of 5 positive affirmations for your life. These areas could include: finances, relationships, health, career opportunities, etc. Be thoughtful and intentional as you create your list. This is not some Christmas wish list but a means for you to activate your own voice and SPEAK into existence the life you want! Practice saying each affirmation daily out loud with strong conviction. Repetition ignites belief and belief leads to action.

_____

_____

_____

_____

_____

_____

_____

_____

_____

_____

_____

FINAL THOUGHT

Through exercising faith, utilizing positive declarations and maintaining an upbeat attitude, I was able to overcome a sudden and life-changing diagnosis of cancer at twenty years old. My journey was not easy, but the experience served a greater purpose. My experience revealed many things to me but two stand out to me the most; to value the gift of life and to trust God's heart even when you can't trace His hand. Recall the quote from the beginning of chapter 5? "Faith is all about believing. You don't know how it will happen. You just know that it will." In 2007, as I was going through difficult months of cancer treatments, I had little control over what I was experiencing in this time of my life. From the initial diagnosis to the type of medical treatments necessary to give me a fighting chance, that aspect of my story was in God's hands.

What I did have control over was my response (attitude) to how I was going to handle this challenge and the decision to remain confident that my healing was inevitable!

No matter what **your** unique story is, no matter what you've been through or how many times you've missed the mark in your life, always make the decision to get back up and continue moving forward. The outcome you experience tomorrow, is determined by the actions you take today. Don't wait for anyone else to motivate you or to hold you accountable for what you need to be doing in your life every day. Ignite your passions and be determined to achieve your greatest dreams! God isn't finished building your incredible story but it's up to you, on how you're going to maximize each day and live ***life on purpose.***

Inside each of us, is the undeniable potential to reach heights unseen if we only take the time to investigate and develop our gifts, talents, faith and courage. Everything you need to **WIN** at life can be found deep within the vaults of your inner-self. Often times, our most significant growth comes in times when our faith is tested and our back is against the wall. Times when our own logic and reasoning doesn't paint a clear picture and we're just not sure how God's going to bring us through 'this one.' It's in these special times when we have to learn how to draw upon the well of faith and strength found deep within a man's soul. In the words of Dr. Kimbro, "It is during these emergencies that we draw upon that secret power from within which knows no resistance great enough to defeat it." It's the boldness of spirit and the endurance of purpose that empowers an individual to overcome just about anything that stands in their way. Take hold of your life and always believe in your abilities. Discover the Champion Inside!

> *"Death is not the greatest loss in life. The greatest loss is what dies inside us while we live."*
>
> —Norman Cousins

FINAL THOUGHT

Win from Within!

For more information and to receive your FREE 7 Steps to Win from Within download, be sure to join Rob's mailing list at http://www.iamrobgadams.com.

Connect with Rob:

 @robgadams

 Rob G. Adams

 @robgadams

REFERENCES

Gross, Gail. *The Important Role of Dad.* 2014.

https://www.huffingtonpost.com/dr-gail-gross/the-important-role-of-dad_b_5489093.html

Terrell, Dontaira. *Overcoming the Crippling Effects of Fear.* 2015.

https://www.huffingtonpost.com/dontaira-terrell-/overcoming-the-crippling-effects-of-fear_b_6931938.html

Kimbro, Dennis. & Hill, Napoleon. *Think and Grow Rich: A Black Choice.* 1992.

LETTERS

"I first met Robert when he came in with his mom for his initial consultation. He was very quiet and calm. He was so patient and just listened. I remember when I was teaching him about what to expect during his treatment, he just listened and said that he trusted in God.

Each week, the doctor would see him to check on how he was doing, and no matter how bad he was feeling, he never complained. Again, he said the God would see him through. His mom would be in the room for these visits, and I only remember one time when he got, "a little impatient" with her as she said he wasn't doing what I recommended. But, even when he was feeling bad he remained calm, smiled and just listened.

He was compliant in doing what he needed to do and I was amazed that a young man like him took responsibility for his care. His attitude remained positive throughout the entire treatment. He didn't say much when he wasn't feeling well, but he always smiled. We all just loved him and he was such an easy patient because of his attitude.

He would ask questions about his prognosis but remained positive and had his plans for what he was going to do when he got better. He recovered quickly and each time we saw him, he would be smiling and would attribute his recovery to his faith.

I rarely meet a young man dealing with cancer who had the strength and optimism as Robert. Treatment for this type of cancer is very difficult. Through it all, I knew he trusted in God as he always said. He continues to do well and he is so patient. It has taken me forever to get this written, and each time he calls, he is as polite as he was from the day I met him."

Primary RN (Falls Church, VA)

"I first met Robert when he started his tomotherapy treatment. What a wonderful spirit he had with his strong belief and faith. He would come in with a smile every day even though he was going through difficult treatment. He would always talk about what God was doing for him. He was so right. He did well and continues to do so. I admire his strength and optimism. I will never forget him."

Office Manager (Falls Church, VA)

www.ingramcontent.com/pod-product-compliance
Lightning Source LLC
Chambersburg PA
CBHW052115070526
44584CB00017B/2496